Zoom in on ROAD MAPS

Kathy Furgang

Enslow Publishing
101 W. 23rd Street
Suite 240
New York, NY 10011
USA
enslow.com

WORDS TO KNOW

compass rose A drawing on a map that shows directions.

highway A main road.

index A list, usually found at the back of a map, that states what is on the map and where a location can be found.

innovations Creations of new things.

interstate Connecting more than one state.

legend A box on a map that explains what the symbols on the map mean.

navigate To make one's way from one place to another.

route The path a person takes to get somewhere.

satellites Spacecraft that circle Earth.

scale The measurements on a map compared to actual measurements in the real world.

CONTENTS

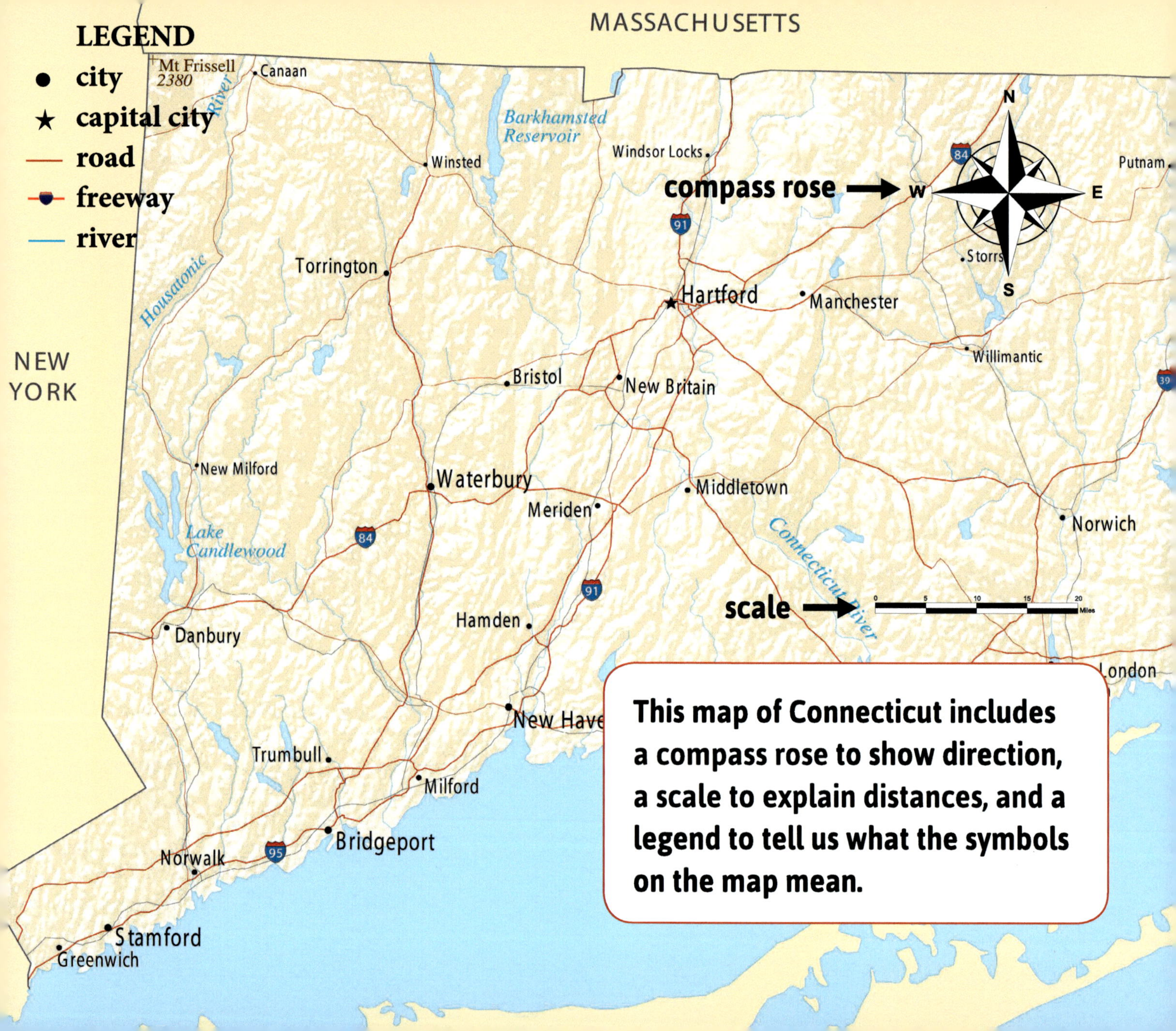

This map of Connecticut includes a compass rose to show direction, a scale to explain distances, and a legend to tell us what the symbols on the map mean.

All About Maps

When you need to find your way from one place to another, what tool do you reach for? A map, of course! A map is an illustration of a place. Most maps have a legend to explain the symbols that are used on the map. Maps also usually have a scale. A scale tells you how the distances on the map compare with distances in the real world. Finally, most maps have a compass rose. A compass rose shows you the four main directions. They are north, south, east, and west. This book will teach you how to use a road map.

Border Lines

Many maps include more than the legend, scale, and compass rose. Maps may also include lines that show borders between states and countries.

The Legend

A legend helps you understand the symbols on a map. There are three main types of symbols. Points stand for places such as cities or towns. Area symbols show larger things, such as lakes. For example, a lake would be an area

Look at the legend in the lower right corner. It explains that point symbols stand for cities and lines show where borders are.

colored in blue. Line symbols are used to stand for roads, railroads, or rivers.

The Scale

A map shows part of the world. It is printed on a paper or shown on a computer. To be able to show something so large in a small space, mapmakers use a scale. The scale is a line with bars and numbers written at either end. The scale shows that an actual distance is equal to a certain length on the map. So, for example, 1 inch on a map might stand for 10 miles in the real world.

Understanding Road Maps

There is a special kind of map made just for drivers. It is called a road map. A road map shows the names of roads and streets in an area. Road maps help you navigate, or drive in the correct direction. You can find your location on a road map and choose the best route to get where you are going. Roads maps can also show natural physical features to help

you better understand the area through which you are traveling.

People may keep printed road maps of their city or state in their car. This can help them find their way if they get lost.

How Much Detail?

Road maps can show different amounts of detail. If the map shows a whole city, for example, it will show the main highways and roads going through the town. It will probably not include every street in the town. There is not enough room for such detail on a city map.

However, a road map of just one neighborhood may be detailed enough to show every street in the area. To find your way from your home to a hotel in another state may mean that you must switch road maps along the way.

Nature's Features

A physical feature on a map is something that is part of the natural landscape. That includes mountains, streams, lakes, and oceans.

A road map of the Los Angeles area shows highways, roads, and other features, like airports.

You may start with one that shows main highways. Then you may have to switch to one with more detail as you get closer to where you are going.

Road Map Features

To understand how a road map works, it helps to get familiar with the different features. The map's legend is usually in a box on the side of a map. Many symbols in the legend are the same from map to map. Major roads like interstate highways are usually labeled with thick red lines. Other roads, like state highways, are shown with a thinner red line. Even smaller roads may be labeled with thin black lines. Dirt roads may be shown as broken lines. It can be hard to understand all these

This map of the Boston area shows the different roads that lead to the city and the towns that surround it.

lines crossing over each other. The basic rule is the thicker the line, the bigger the road.

Map Direction

Remember that a compass rose shows the directions on a map. Look at the road map of Florida on the next page. Find the compass rose. The arrows are labeled N, S, E, and W to stand for north, south, east, and west.

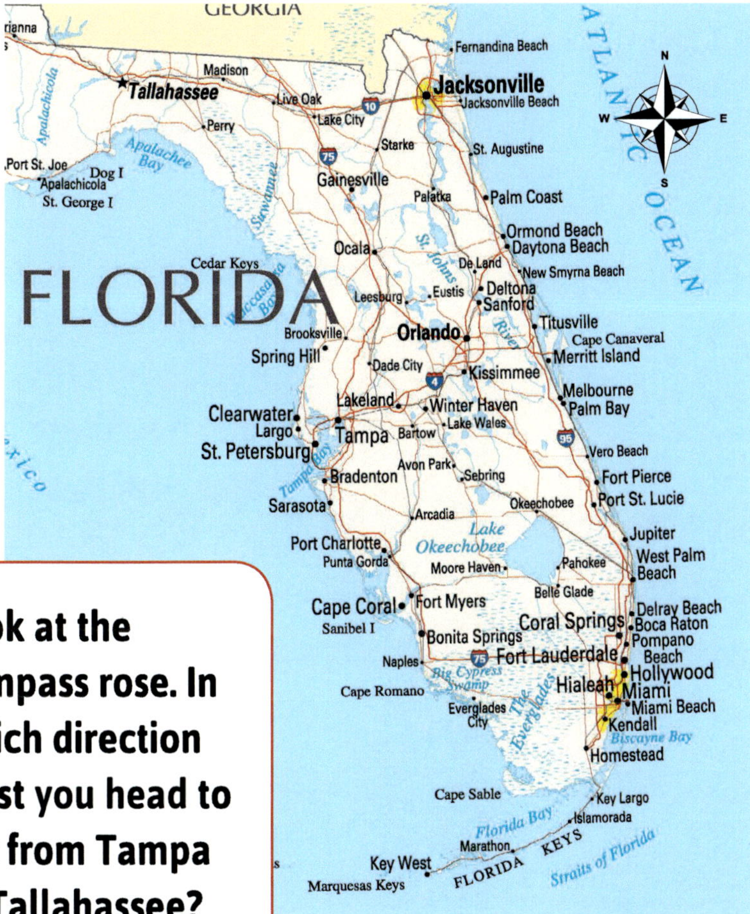

Look at the compass rose. In which direction must you head to get from Tampa to Tallahassee?

Using directions, we can compare the positions of two cities. Find the cities of Jacksonville and Orlando on the map. Jacksonville is near the top of the map, and Orlando is near the middle. If you place your finger on Jacksonville and slide your finger toward Orlando, you move your finger down. Moving down on the map is south. This means that Orlando is south of Jacksonville.

How to Use the Index

An index can help you find what you are looking for on a map. An index lists different locations. Each location is a combination of a letter and a number. These letters and numbers are arranged on the edge of the map. Practice using an index with the map of Ohio on page 17.

Navigating the Seas

The compass rose has been used on maps since the 1300s. It was used mainly by sailors to tell which way the winds were blowing.

Road Map Features

INDEX

A

Akron F-2

Alliance F-2

Ashland E-2

Athens E-5

B

Barberton E-2

Beavercreek B-4

Bellefontaine C-3

Bucyrus D-2

Using the index on this road map of Ohio, look up Bellefontaine. It is located at C-3. The letter C is on the top of the map, and the number 3 is on the side. Trace a finger from C and a finger from 3 until your fingers meet. You have found Bellefontaine!

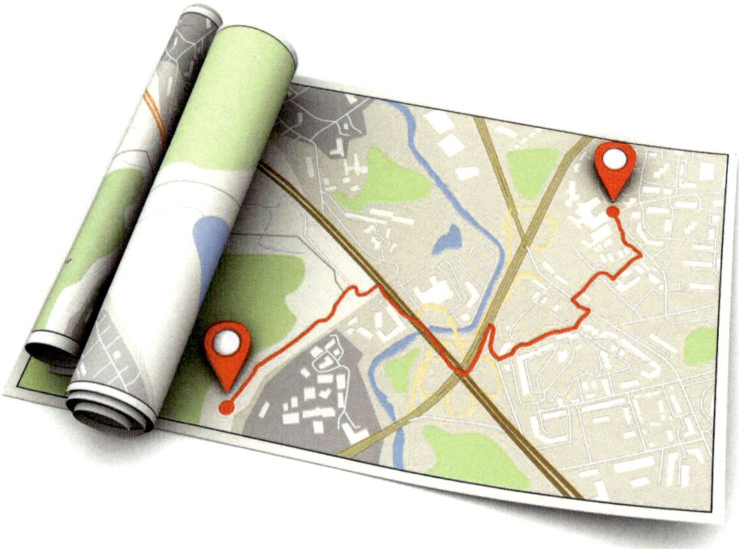

Uses for Road Maps

People have been using road maps for nearly as long as there have been cars on the road. Road maps are useful for many things. They can help you plan a trip. You can use the map to write down the directions you should take from one place to another. Road maps can even help you find places like restaurants or gas stations. You can use the legend to find out how long your trip will take. You can use it to plan stops along the way.

The details on a road map can be very helpful when planning a trip.

Road maps can also be used to help you find another route on your trip. You can avoid construction or traffic by using a road map.

Help from Satellites

There have been innovations in mapping. GPS is a tool that helps travelers plan their routes. GPS stands for Global Positioning System. It shows users exactly where they are located. GPS works by using satellites. The

Satellite Signals

Satellites are spacecraft that orbit, or circle, Earth. They send and receive signals for communication, weather, and navigation, or finding a position along a route. The United States military has used satellite technology since the 1960s. They have been available in cars since around 2000.

satellites send information to the GPS tool that tells a user his or her exact location. Sometimes a GPS can even display a road map on its screen. This is a different way to use a road map. By using a GPS tool in addition to using the map-reading skills you have learned, you can plan trips faster and better than ever before.

GPS is a very useful tool for drivers. It can give directions to a location and can even warn a driver if there is traffic or an accident ahead.

ACTIVITY: TAKE A ROAD TRIP

Look at the road map to the right. Answer each question using the legend, compass rose, and scale on the left to help you.

1. Find the capital of Wyoming. What highway runs through it?
2. You are in the town of Riverton. In which direction must you drive to get to Jackson Lake?
3. Which is the best highway to take to get from Casper to Buffalo?
4. About how far is it from Rock Springs to Farson?

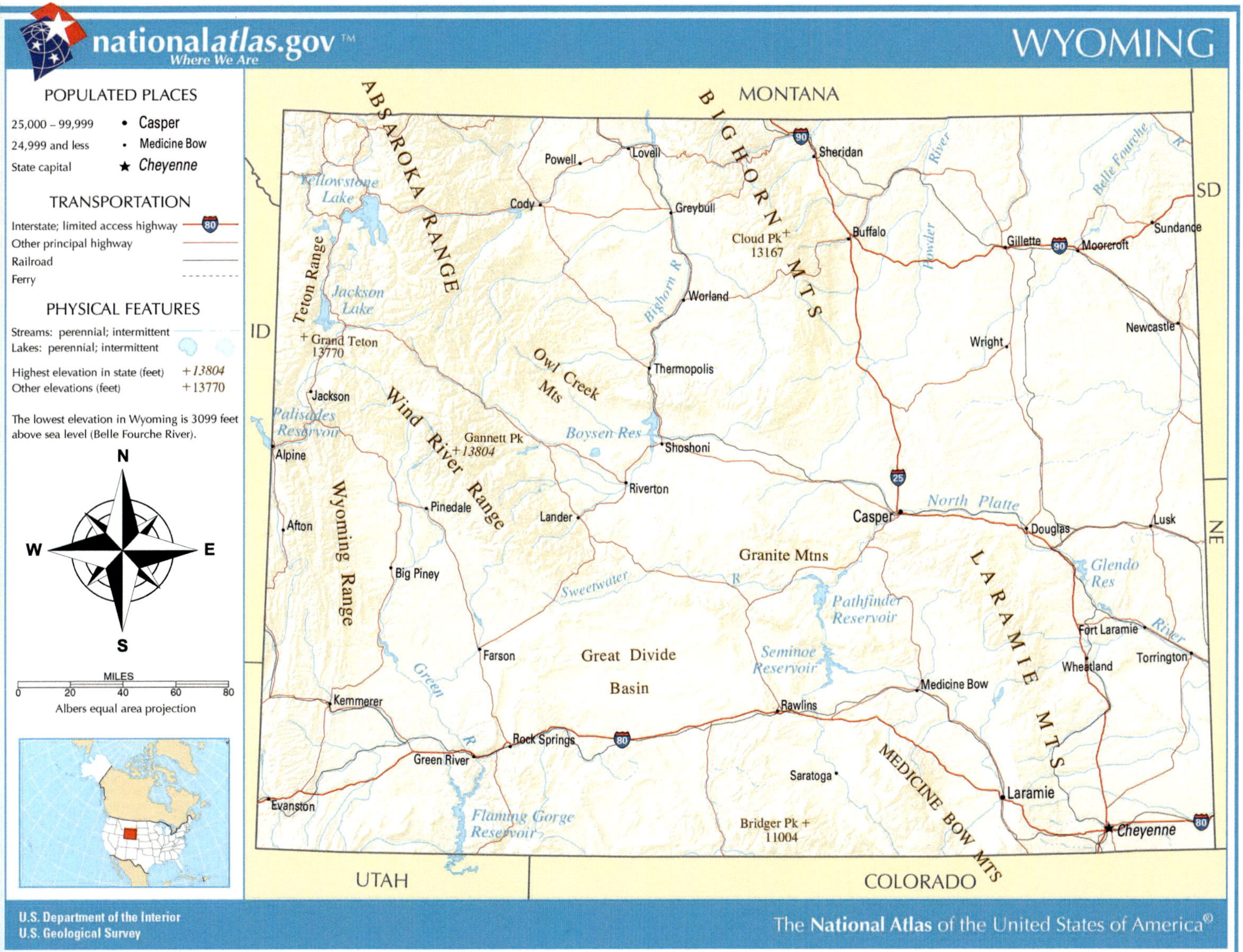

pagegen_wy3.pdf INTERIOR-GEOLOGICAL SURVEY, RESTON, VIRGINIA-200

LEARN MORE

Books

Balkan, Gabrielle. ***The 50 States: Explore the U.S.A. with 50 Fact-filled Maps!*** New York, NY: Wide Eyed Editions, 2015.

Mizielinska, Aleksandra, and Daniel Mizielinski. ***Maps***. Somerville, MA: Big Picture Press, 2013.

Smithsonian Children's Illustrated Atlas. London, UK: Dorling Kindersley, 2016.

Websites

BrainPop Jr.

jr.brainpop.com/socialstudies/geography/readingmaps/

Play games and take quizzes as you learn to read maps.

National Geographic Kids Atlases

www.nationalgeographic.com/kids-world-atlas/maps.html

Learn about different types of maps by exploring them interactively.

INDEX

Published in 2018 by Enslow Publishing, LLC.
101 W. 23rd Street, Suite 240, New York, NY 10011

Library of Congress Cataloging-in-Publication Data

Names: Furgang, Kathy.
Title: Zoom in on road maps / Kathy Furgang.
Description: New York : Enslow Publishing, 2018 | Series: Zoom in on maps | Includes bibliographical references and index. | Audience: K to Grade 3.
Identifiers: ISBN 9780766092235 (library bound) | ISBN 9780766094307 (pbk.) | ISBN 9780766094314 (6 pack)
Subjects: LCSH: Roads—Maps—Juvenile literature. | Map reading—Juvenile literature.
Classification: LCC GA130. F88 2018 | DDC 912.01/4—dc23

Printed in China

To Our Readers: We have done our best to make sure all website addresses in this book were active and appropriate when we went to press. However, the author and the publisher have no control over and assume no liability for the material available on those websites or on any websites they may link to. Any comments or suggestions can be sent by email to customerservice@enslow.com.

Portions of this book originally appeared in *Road Maps* by Ian Mahaney.

Photos Credits: Cover, p. 1 Stephen VanHorn/Shutterstock.com; cover, p. 1 (background) pop_jop/DigitalVision Vectors/Getty Images; pp. 2, 3, 22, back cover Artfury/Shutterstock.com; pp. 4, 14, 15, 17, 23 National Atlas of the United States, http://nationalatlas.gov; pp. 5, 9, 13, 18 Mmaxer/Shutterstock.com; pp. 6, 8, 16, 20 Artfury/Shutterstock.com; p. 7 Encyclopaedia Britannica/Universal Images Group/Getty Images; p. 10 Denis Rozhnovsky/Shutterstock.com; p. 12 ©2002 GeoAtlas; p. 19 Rawpixel.com/Shutterstock.com; p. 21 Syda Productions/Shutterstock.com.